Published by Sourcebooks, Inc.
P.O. Box 4410, Naperville, Illinois 60567-4410
(630) 961-3900
Fax: (630) 961-2168
www.sourcebooks.com

Originally published in the United Kingdom by Bantam Press, an imprint of Transworld Publishers

Printed and bound in China.

10 9 8 7 6 5 4 3 2 1

Love is me saying it again on this page.

Waldo Pancake

I love you so much that I went into a shop and bought you a little book about it.

They should make a film about our life together. Minus the watching-TV-on-the-sofa-most-of-the-time bit.

Me

You

society's
pressures

You can fold
my corner
over any
time.

I love it when you use my pockets as a bin for your chocolate wrappers, etc.

Absence makes the choosing what to watch on TV much easier.

Let's paint the town red.

I've just thought this through and realized how much hassle it'd be.

When we have a hug,
I always imagine you're
doing one of those looks
over my shoulder like in
a soap opera, hence me
always hugging you when
we're between two mirrors.

You bring out the **schmaltz** in me.

You had
whatev
you said

ne at
r it was

Would it be weird if I had you stuffed if you died first?

I'm not saying I love your snoring, but the fact that it doesn't make me want to strangle you speaks volumes.

You know when you se
each other's eyes an
and it makes you wa

Tha

couple looking into

ggling and canoodling

b be sick?

's us.

You bring out the best in me*

*worst might also be brought out.

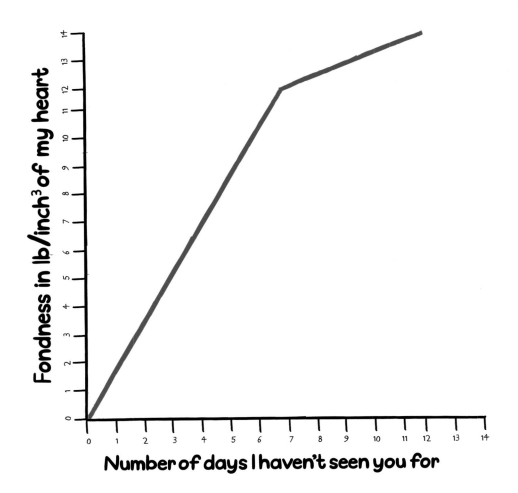

no pressure
there then ——————→

You're my
reason
for li♥ing.

How ironic would it be if you threw this book at me during a fight.

You a
grea

e the
est*

*no scientific proof of this.

I like to imagine us as a really old couple, walking along the street with our canes, holding hands. Although we'll probably have shopping bags in our spare hands. Saying that, we'll be doing our shopping on the internet by then, won't we. Amazing isn't it.

I've read the book*

*what you can say now when subject of love comes up.

You know how couples are always picking bits of fluff off each other's sweaters?

That's why single people are so fluffy.

I love you even more than **me**

I saw one of your socks on the floor and I felt the same love for it that I do for you.

How sad would it be if
I was in a charity shop
after we'd split up or
whatev and I saw this
book on the shelf.

Have you seen those little birds on nature shows that decorate their nests then dance around, trying to attract a mate?

That was me that time when I tidied up my apartment at the beginning of our relationship.

LL

Imagine if "hate" meant "love" and vice versa. I reckon there'd be loads more people saying they loved each other.

People always say "fall in love," which makes me think of someone falling, and how they look terrified.

You know when I'm not listening to what you're saying? That's because I'm too busy thinking about you.

Weird that if we hadn't met I'd be giving this book to someone else.

(Pretend I didn't just think that then write it down and get it printed.)

I only have eyes for you.

And TV.

I had a massive
wave of love
for you today.
It's gone now.

Love is me immediately
thinking you've moved
whatever it is I'm
looking for.

IF I GOT **LOVE** TATTOOED ONTO MY FOREHEAD IN TRIBUTE TO OUR RELATIONSHIP WOULD IT BE WEIRD?

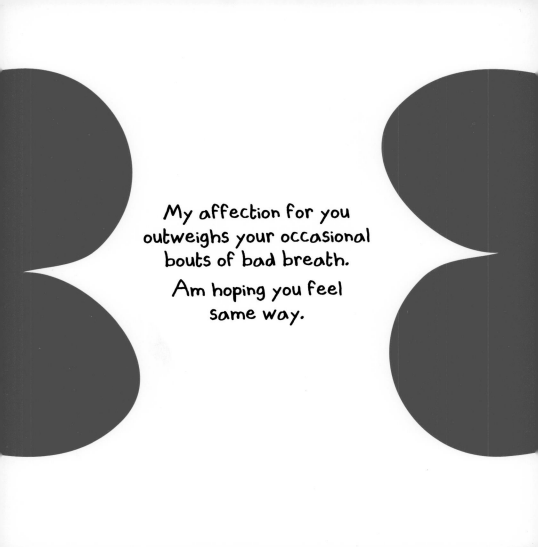

My affection for you
outweighs your occasional
bouts of bad breath.

Am hoping you feel
same way.

Hi, this is the author. I'd just like to point out that it's me writing all this stuff, not the person who bought it for you.

You say tomato,
I go to the fridge
and get you one.

I've contemplated the whole scattering petals thing. Is that good enough for you?

Canoodle,
willoodle.

I love you
to bits.

$\longrightarrow$

eye x2   kidney x2
nose   spleen
ear x2   shoulder x2
mouth   neck
leg x2   elbow x2
arm x2   palm x2
nipple x2   bum
thumb x2   thigh x2
fingers x8   etc.
knee x2
ankle x2
heart
liver
lung x2

you

My
better
half →

Stick
photo of
loved
one here*

*not gonna happen.

Weird how adding poo
to something makes it
more lovey-dovey.

Like, "How's my darling
poopoo today?"

It just workypoos.

When I put my arm round you, sometimes it's to rest my arm.

Brilliant, another person for me to worry about dying.

You know when you're talking and it's like I'm looking right through you? That's because eyes are the windows to your soul, and I'm staring right at it,

BABY.

Have you seen my book about VOLEs? It's like this one, but with V & L swapped round.

If you were a book review it'd be overwhelmingly positive.

(massive
close-up
of heart)

Completely
and utterly
loved out.

Coming soon

Hate is buying book.

me not
you this

You and
me'll
never end.